Aircraft Carriers

by Michael Green

Content Consultant:
Jack A. Green, Historian
Naval Historical Center

CAPSTONE PRESS
MANKATO, MINNESOTA

C A P S T O N E P R E S S

818 North Willow Street • Mankato, Minnesota 56001
http://www.capstone-press.com

Printed in the United States of America.

Library of Congress Cataloging-in-Publication Data
Green, Michael, 1952-
    Aircraft carriers/by Michael Green.
    p. cm. -- (Land and sea)
    Includes bibliographical references and index.
    Summary: An introduction to the ships known as "floating airports," from their inception in the early twentieth century, through their development during World War II, to the various classes of carriers in use today.
    ISBN 1-56065-553-4
    1. Aircraft carriers--United States--Juvenile literature. [1. Aircraft carriers.] I. Title. II. Series: Land and sea (Mankato, Minn.)

V874.3.G74 1998
623.8'255--dc21

                                           97-7755
                                            CIP

                                             AC

Editorial credits
Editor, Timothy Larson; Cover design, Timothy Halldin; Illustrations, James Franklin; Photo Research Assistant, Michelle L. Norstad
Photo credits
U.S. Navy, cover, 4, 6, 8, 11, 12, 15, 17, 18, 20, 24, 26, 28, 30, 33, 34, 36, 37, 38, 41, 47

Table of Contents

Chapter 1

Aircraft Carriers

Aircraft carriers are large warships that carry airplanes. A warship is a ship with guns or other weapons that navies use for war. Aircraft carriers are so large that they are like airports that go to sea. Many people call aircraft carriers, carriers.

The most important job of aircraft carriers is launching planes. Launch means to set into action. During wartime, carriers and other warships work together as a battle group.

Crews of sailors and pilots run aircraft carriers. A pilot is a person who flies planes. Some pilots fly planes off aircraft carriers. They also land planes on carriers. Sailors refuel and repair planes on aircraft carriers. Other sailors control the ship.

The U.S. Navy named its first aircraft carrier after a man important to the study of flying. Until

An aircraft carrier is a large warship that carries planes.

The top decks on carriers are similar to airport runways.

1963, the U.S. Navy named its other carriers after historic warships and battles. In 1963, the navy started naming its carriers after U.S. presidents and other important people.

The U.S. Navy puts carriers that are alike into groups called classes. Sometimes, a class has only one ship in it. The navy names each class after the first ship in the group. The navy creates a new class for each new kind of carrier it commissions. A commission is a navy order to put a ship into service.

Aircraft Carrier Form

Every aircraft carrier has the same basic form. The hull of an aircraft carrier looks like other large ships. A hull is a ship's frame. A carrier has an anchor in the bow. The bow is the front of a ship. Propellers called screws are located in the stern. The stern is the rear of a ship.

An aircraft carrier is divided into decks. The first deck is the top deck. People can see the top deck from outside. Sailors call the top deck, topside. Other decks lie below the top deck.

The top deck of an aircraft carrier is different from other ships. The top deck on a carrier is similar to an airport runway. Because of this, the navy calls the top deck of a carrier the flight deck. Planes use the flight deck to take off and land.

The Flight Deck and the Superstructure

Planes usually need long runways to take off and to land safely. Airport runways are long for this reason. But the flight decks on aircraft carriers are shorter than airport runways.

Carrier planes need help taking off and landing because of the short runways. On carrier flight decks, catapults help planes take off. Arresting wires help them land. A catapult is a device like a slingshot. It

A carrier's planes are stored on the hangar deck, located below flight deck.

launches planes off the end of a flight deck. Arresting wires help planes stop quickly as they land. Arresting wires lie across the flight deck. Planes drag hooks as they land, which catch the wires. This helps stop the planes.

Each carrier has a control tower called a superstructure located on the flight deck. Sailors on carriers call the superstructure the island. The island contains the bridge. The bridge is where the captain controls the ship. Sailors also direct a carrier's planes from the island. A carrier's radar is on the island, too. Radar is a type of machinery that uses radio waves to locate and guide things.

The Lower Decks

Sailors call the lower decks, below. The deck below the flight deck is called the hangar deck. A hangar is a place where planes are stored. Each carrier's hangar deck has one or more hangars. Sailors fix planes and arm planes in the hangars.

Each deck has many rooms called compartments. Some compartments are for sleeping. Some are for cooking and eating. Some compartments are for equipment. Other compartments make up a small hospital for sailors who get hurt.

A carrier's boilers and turbines are in compartments called engine rooms. A boiler is a special kind of heater. It makes steam to power a turbine. A turbine is an engine. A turbine provides the power to turn the screws that make a carrier move.

Size, Weight, Speed, and Distance

The U.S. Navy's first aircraft carrier was its smallest. The carrier was 534 feet (160 meters) long. Today, navy carriers are so large that they are as long as some skyscrapers are tall. The navy's newest carrier is 1,096 feet (329 meters) long.

Displacement describes the weight of ships. Displacement is the weight of the water that a ship pushes away from itself while afloat. A ship's displacement can change depending on the load it carries.

The smallest U.S. Navy carriers displace about 20,000 tons (18,000 metric tons) of water. Today's carriers are the largest in navy history. The largest of these carriers displaces 97,000 tons (87,300 metric tons) of water.

People measure the speed of ships and boats in knots. One knot is 1.15 miles per hour. The fastest navy carriers can travel at speeds up to 35 knots. This is about 40 miles (64 kilometers) per hour.

Weapons

Many aircraft carriers have small guns for protection. These guns are antiaircraft guns. Antiaircraft guns are used to shoot at attacking planes. Antiaircraft guns are usually located on the carriers' control towers and their flight decks.

An aircraft carrier's best weapons are its planes.

An aircraft carrier's best weapons are its planes. The ship's planes have weapons to attack the enemy. The planes carry guns and different kinds of explosives. These explosives can be bombs, missiles, and torpedoes. A missile is an explosive that can fly long distances. A torpedo is an explosive that travels underwater.

Chapter 2

Early Carrier History

The U.S. Navy tested the idea for making aircraft carriers in 1910. A pilot flew a plane off the rear deck of a U.S. Navy cruiser. A cruiser is a medium-sized warship. In the same year, the pilot landed a plane on a navy cruiser.

The British navy also did similar tests at the end of World War I (1914-1918). U.S. Navy officers watched these tests. The U.S. Navy saw the benefits of building a ship to carry planes. In 1922, the U.S. Navy changed the supply ship *Jupiter* into its first aircraft carrier. The navy named it the *Langley* in honor of airplane pioneer Samuel T. Langley.

A plane landed on a ship for the first time in 1910.

The *Langley*

The *Langley* was a test carrier. The U.S. Navy used it to see if building more aircraft carriers was a good idea. It looked different than modern aircraft carriers. There was no island on the *Langley*'s flight deck. The *Langley* also had an open-sided hangar deck.

The flight deck on the *Langley* was 534 feet (162 meters) long. The ship had a top speed of 15 knots. The *Langley* carried 468 pilots and sailors and 34 planes.

The first plane took off from the *Langley* on October 17, 1922. Reports do not show where the plane landed. The navy believes the plane landed on shore. The first recorded landing on the *Langley* took place nine days later. A different plane made the landing.

Japanese bomber planes attacked the *Langley* during World War II (1939-1945). The ship caught on fire during the battle. The *Langley*'s crew had to abandon the ship, and it sank.

The First Large U.S. Navy Carriers

The *Langley* proved that planes could take off and land on ships. In 1927, the U.S. Navy commissioned its first large aircraft carriers. The

The *Langley* was the U.S. Navy's first aircraft carrier.

navy built its first two large carriers by adding flight decks to cruiser hulls.

The navy named the carriers the *Lexington* and the *Saratoga*. Sailors saw that the carriers' flight decks covered up their hangar decks. Many sailors nicknamed the carriers covered wagons because of this.

The *Lexington* and the *Saratoga* were 890 feet (267 meters) long. They remained the navy's largest carriers up to the late 1940s. The new carriers each displaced 33,000 tons (29,700 metric tons) of water.

Both new carriers could carry 83 planes and had crews of 2,000 people. This is enough people to make up a small town. The top speed of the ships was almost 35 knots. At that time, they were the fastest large ships in the world.

More Carriers

The *Lexington* and the *Saratoga* were useful warships for the U.S. Navy. The navy planned to build more aircraft carriers. The navy wanted to find the best size and speed for its carriers.

The navy commissioned the small carrier *Ranger* in 1934. The *Ranger* was a navy experiment with small carriers. It was 769 feet long. This made it 121 feet (36 meters) shorter than the *Lexington* and the *Saratoga*. Through tests, the navy learned the *Ranger* was not useful for battle. The ship was too small to handle rough seas or serve in battle groups. The navy used the carrier mainly as a training ship.

By the mid-1930s, the navy wanted a carrier bigger than the *Ranger*, but smaller than the *Lexington*. In 1936, the navy commissioned the *Yorktown* and the *Enterprise*. They were both in the Yorktown class. They each were 809 feet

The *Lexington* had a top speed of 35 knots.

(247 meters) long. Both ships had a top speed of
32 knots.

In 1939, the navy commissioned the *Wasp*.
The *Wasp* was the navy's attempt to make another
small carrier. It was 688 feet (206 meters) long.
This made it smaller than the *Ranger*. The ship's
design was based on the *Yorktown*. The navy
hoped this design would make the small carrier

The *Hornet* was an improved Yorktown class carrier.

useful. But it handled poorly and did not hold up well under battle.

The navy commissioned the *Hornet* in 1940. The ship was an improved Yorktown class carrier. The *Hornet* had a slightly larger flight deck and better armor than the *Yorktown*. Armor is a protective metal covering.

U.S. Carriers at War

The U.S. Navy's aircraft carriers fought in many battles during World War II. The United States entered the war when Japanese planes attacked Pearl Harbor on December 7, 1941. The planes sank or damaged much of the U.S. Navy's Pacific Fleet in the harbor. A fleet is a group of warships under one command.

But none of the fleet's aircraft carriers were in the harbor that day. The navy depended on these carriers to fight the Japanese during World War II. Within 10 months, four of the navy's carriers sank during battle.

The *Lexington* was the first aircraft carrier to sink. In May 1942, five Japanese torpedoes hit the ship during the Battle of the Coral Sea. A gasoline leak caused a series of explosions that destroyed the ship.

The *Yorktown* sank during the Battle of Midway in June 1942. In September 1942, a Japanese submarine made a surprise attack on the *Wasp*. A submarine is a warship that can travel both on top of water and underwater. The *Wasp*

The *Enterprise* fought in more major battles than any other U.S. Navy carrier during World War II.

was launching scout planes when the submarine attacked. The attack damaged the ship, and it sank.

Japanese planes sank the *Hornet* during the Battle of Santa Cruz in October 1942. The navy reused the *Hornet*'s name for a new Essex class carrier in 1944.

The *Enterprise*

Only three of the U.S. Navy's original aircraft carriers survived the sea battles of 1942. The most famous was the *Enterprise*. Sailors nicknamed the carrier Old Lady because the ship survived so many battles.

The *Enterprise* carried 18 fighter planes, 36 dive bombers, and 18 torpedo bombers. The *Enterprise* also had more than 40 antiaircraft guns to defend itself from enemy planes.

Each kind of plane had a job to do during battle. Fighter planes defended the carrier from enemy planes. They also attacked enemy ships and other targets. Bomber planes dropped bombs on enemy ships and targets on land. Torpedo bombers attacked enemy ships by dropping torpedoes in the water.

The *Enterprise* fought in more major battles than any other navy ship. During 1942, planes from the *Enterprise* sank 35 Japanese ships. These planes also shot down 185 Japanese aircraft.

In 1945, Japanese planes badly damaged the *Enterprise*. Then the navy used the ship to transport soldiers. The navy removed the *Enterprise* from service in 1947.

Replacement Carriers

In late 1942, the U.S. Navy realized it needed more carriers to fight World War II. At the time, the navy was building a new class of carriers. But these carriers would not be ready until 1944. The navy needed carriers right away.

The navy solved the problem by changing nine unfinished cruisers into aircraft carriers. The navy fitted the ships with flight decks and hangars. Then the navy sent the ships into battle.

These new carriers were the Independence class. They had a top speed of 30 knots and could carry up to 45 planes. Each of these carriers was 600 feet (180 meters) long. They each had crews made up of 1,500 sailors and pilots.

The navy also changed some supply ships into small aircraft carriers. The new ships were the Escort class carriers. These carriers led groups of ships and carried planes to where they were needed.

By the end of 1943, the navy had changed more than 50 ships into carriers. These carriers helped the navy and its allies fight many battles and campaigns in the Pacific Ocean. Allies are countries that help one another. A campaign is a series of battles.

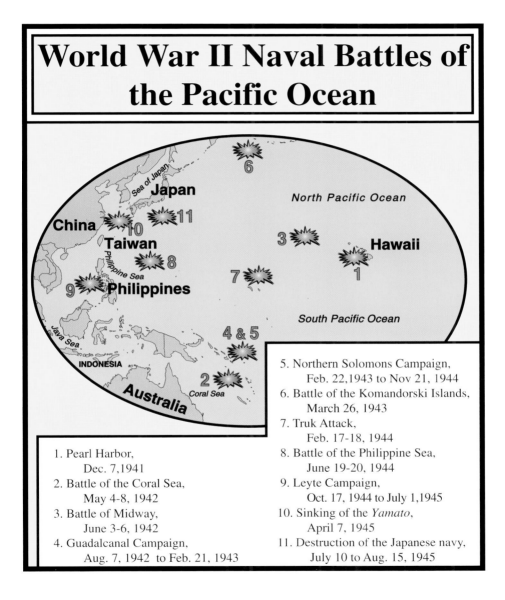

World War II Naval Battles of the Pacific Ocean

1. Pearl Harbor,
   Dec. 7, 1941
2. Battle of the Coral Sea,
   May 4-8, 1942
3. Battle of Midway,
   June 3-6, 1942
4. Guadalcanal Campaign,
   Aug. 7, 1942 to Feb. 21, 1943
5. Northern Solomons Campaign,
   Feb. 22, 1943 to Nov 21, 1944
6. Battle of the Komandorski Islands,
   March 26, 1943
7. Truk Attack,
   Feb. 17-18, 1944
8. Battle of the Philippine Sea,
   June 19-20, 1944
9. Leyte Campaign,
   Oct. 17, 1944 to July 1, 1945
10. Sinking of the *Yamato*,
    April 7, 1945
11. Destruction of the Japanese navy,
    July 10 to Aug. 15, 1945

Chapter 3

Recent Carrier History

The U.S. Navy finished 17 new aircraft carriers in 1944. The navy put these ships in the Essex class. The navy built six more Essex class carriers before the end of World War II.

Essex class carriers were large ships. The first Essex class carriers had wooden flight decks that were 820 feet (246 meters) long. Later carriers in the class had flight decks up to 854 feet (256 meters) long.

Steel frameworks supported the wooden flight decks on Essex class carriers. Each ship also had an armored hangar deck. The armor protected the sailors and planes on the decks below.

Essex class carriers had wooden flight decks.

Each ship's hangar deck was connected to the flight deck by open-sided elevators. The elevators were so large they could lift planes up to the flight deck. The Essex class carriers had three elevators. Today's carriers still have these large elevators.

Essex class carriers could carry up to 90 planes and had crew sizes of nearly 3,500 people. Each Essex class carrier had 132 antiaircraft guns.

The Essex class carriers displaced about 27,000 tons (24,300 metric tons) of water. They were powered by large turbine engines. Each of these carriers could reach a top speed of 30 knots.

Essex class carriers were very important to U.S. Navy battles in the Pacific Ocean. These carriers fought in many battles during 1945.

Preserved Essex Class Carriers

After World War II, the U.S. Navy did not need the Essex class carriers. Most of the Essex class carriers went into storage between 1947 and 1948. Only the six newest Essex class carriers remained in service.

Today's carriers have open-sided elevators like those on the Essex class carriers of the 1940s.

Planes often had accidents when landing on the flight decks of older carriers.

The navy brought the older Essex class carriers out of storage during the Korean War (1950-1953). The navy had to improve the older carriers to make them useful.

After the Korean War, most of the ships remained in service until they became worn out. Five of the 23 carriers remained in service into the 1980s. One Essex class carrier remained in service into the early 1990s.

The navy sold many of the ships for their parts as the ships left service. But the navy preserved four of the carriers. The *Yorktown*, the *Intrepid*, and the *Lexington* are now public museums. The new *Hornet* is still in storage. Eventually, it may become a museum, too.

The Midway Class Carriers

In the late 1940s, the navy commissioned the Midway class carriers to replace the older Essex class carriers. Between 1955 and 1957, the navy fitted the carriers with angled flight decks.

Older carriers had one long, straight flight deck. Planes took off from the front of the flight deck. Returning planes landed on the rear of the flight deck. Sometimes they crashed or ran into the planes at the front of the flight deck. These accidents killed many people and destroyed many planes.

Angled flight decks added extra runway space on these and all later carriers. Planes took off from the front. Returning planes landed on the angled runway. Today's carriers have angled flight decks.

Midway class carriers were 900 feet (270 meters) long. At the time, this made them the navy's largest carriers. Turbine engines powered

The U.S. Navy calls its largest carriers, super carriers.

the large carriers and gave them a top of speed of 33 knots. They carried crews of 3,500 sailors and pilots and up to 137 planes.

Forrestal Class Super Carriers

Between 1952 and 1959, the navy built four large aircraft carriers for the Forrestal class. These ships were 990 feet (297 meters) long with main flight decks of more than 1,039 feet (312 meters) long. Since the 1950s, the U.S. Navy has called its largest carriers, super carriers.

Forrestal class carriers were the first carriers that the navy built for jet planes. Each carrier had 80 or more planes. These carriers were also the first carriers that the navy fitted with steam-powered catapults. During daylight, their long runways and powerful catapults allowed four jets to take off every minute.

The Forrestal class carriers carried crews of 4,676 sailors and pilots. Each carrier displaced almost 80,000 tons (72,000 metric tons) of water. The carriers were powered by turbine engines and had a top speed of 30 knots or more.

Replacement Carriers

The navy was also working on the Kitty Hawk class carriers by the late 1950s. The navy wanted the most modern ships. The navy replaced the Forrestal class carriers with carriers in the Kitty Hawk class.

These new ships are not much larger than the Forrestal class carriers. They displace 82,000 tons (73,000 metric tons) of water. They have top speeds of 30 to 32 knots.

Kitty Hawk class carriers have angled flight decks and carry 80 planes or more. The ships also carry more than 5,500 sailors. One-half of these sailors take care of the planes. The navy removed the last of these ships from service in 1996.

Nuclear-Powered Super Carriers

In 1961, the U.S. Navy commissioned its first aircraft carrier with nuclear-powered turbine engines. Nuclear power is a powerful kind of energy that lasts longer than other kinds of energy. The fuel for these engines is nuclear rods. Rods are nuclear-charged metal bars.

The navy named the new aircraft carrier the *Enterprise* after the famous World War II carrier. Since the early 1960s, the navy has named many carriers after famous ships as an honor. The new *Enterprise* is still in service today.

The hull of the new *Enterprise* is based on the Forrestal class hulls. However, its hull is 1,040 feet (312 meters) long. This makes it 60 feet (18 meters) longer than any Forrestal class carrier.

The new *Enterprise* displaces almost 90,000 tons (81,000 metric tons) of water. It has a top

The new *Enterprise* can carry up to 80 planes, like these F-14 Tomcats.

speed of 30 knots or more. Like the Forrestal class carriers, the new *Enterprise* can carry 80 planes or more.

The new *Enterprise*'s nuclear-powered turbines allow it to go without refueling for up to 15 years. Carriers with turbine engines need to be refueled every few days. Nuclear-powered

The Nimitz class carriers are still in service today.

carriers like the new *Enterprise* are only limited by the need for supplies.

The Nimitz Class Super Carriers

In 1975, the navy commissioned a new class of nine nuclear-powered carriers. They are known as the Nimitz class carriers. These carriers are still in service today.

The Nimitz class carriers are nearly the same size as the new *Enterprise*. The ships range in length from 1,040 to 1,092 feet (312 to 328 meters). Some of the carriers in this class displace as much as 97,500 tons (87,750 metric tons) of water. They can reach top speeds of 30 to 32 knots.

Nimitz class carriers have crews of 5,500 people and carry 90 of the best military planes. Some of these planes are deadly F/A-18 Hornets. The navy uses these planes to attack many enemy targets. Some are fighter jets. Their job is to defend the aircraft carriers. Others are scout planes and helicopters. A helicopter is an aircraft with rotating blades on its top.

The Nimitz class aircraft carriers were the largest carriers in the world until 1996. At that time, the navy launched the *Harry S. Truman*. The carrier is 1,096 feet (329 meters) long. This makes the carrier as long as New York's Empire State Building is tall.

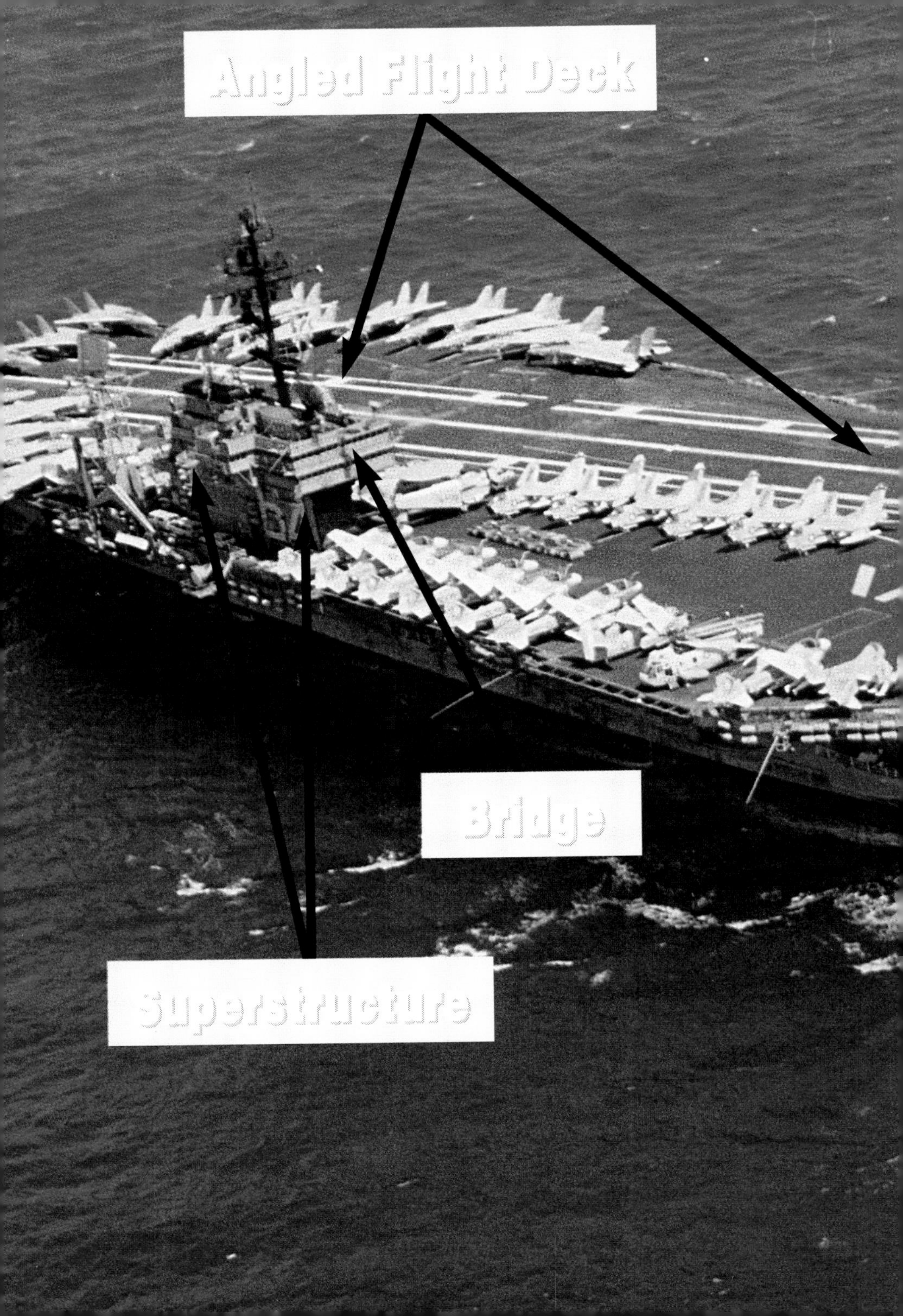

Angled Flight Deck

Bridge

Superstructure

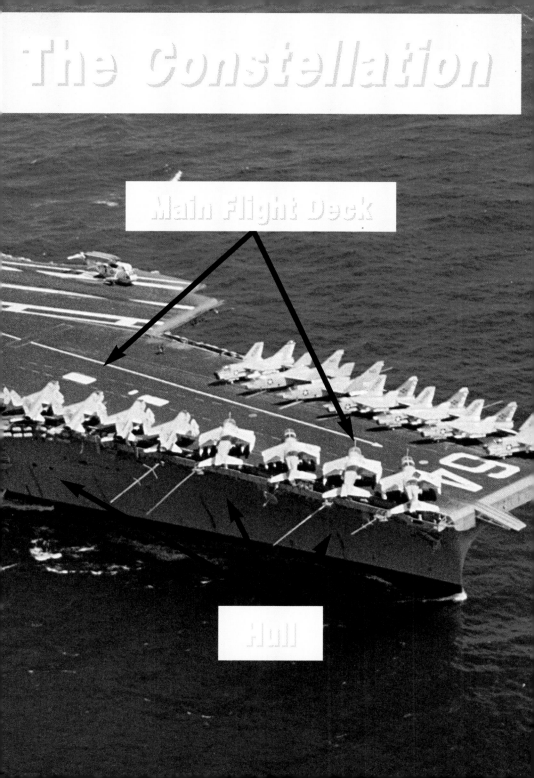

The Constellation

Main Flight Deck

Hull

Chapter 4

Safety and the Future

Today's aircraft carriers are protected by carrier battle groups. Problems can occur on carriers, even with this protection.

Fire is a major concern on an aircraft carrier. A carrier stores a lot of fuel for its planes. This fuel can burn and explode easily. A modern carrier may hold 3 million gallons (11 million liters) of plane fuel.

A modern carrier also has many bombs and missiles for its planes. These bombs could explode because of accidents or enemy attacks.

Safety Features on Carriers

Because of the many dangers, the U.S. Navy builds its carriers with safety features. The most

Carriers are protected by carrier battle groups.

important safety feature on a carrier is its fire-fighting system.

Every modern carrier has water sprinklers as part of its fire-fighting system. The sprinklers are set off by smoke or fire. Crew members can set off the sprinkler system by remote control, too.

A modern carrier also has a lot of fire plugs. A fire plug provides water. Hoses screw onto fire plugs to help aim the water. Sailors learn how to use the fire plugs and hoses to fight fire.

Other Concerns

The fuel that powers today's nuclear-powered carriers is dangerous. The new and used rods are harmful to humans. Sailors must handle and store the rods very carefully.

New weapons also present safety problems for U.S. Navy carriers. A large number of deadly antiship missiles now exist. Aircraft carriers cannot defend against all the new missiles.

Today, there is far less need for aircraft carriers. The Soviet Union broke into smaller countries in 1991. Each country's navy is smaller and less dangerous than the old Soviet navy.

Crew members on carriers learn how to fight fires.

Many of the world's conflicts are now much smaller in size, too.

The U.S. government is limiting the amount of money it gives to the navy. The navy can not operate a lot of carriers because of this lack of money.

Despite these problems, the navy still considers these ships its most valuable warships. No other warship can bring large numbers of planes close to an enemy.

Words to Know

armor (AR-mur)—a protective metal covering
arresting wires (uh-REST-ing WIRES)—wires on the flight deck of an aircraft carrier that help landing planes stop quickly
boiler (BOI-lur)—a special heater that makes steam to power turbines
bridge (BRIJ)—a room where the captain controls a ship
catapult (KAT-uh-puhlt)—a device that launches planes off the end of an aircraft carrier's flight deck
commission (kuh-MISH-uhn)—a navy order to put a ship into service
fleet (FLEET)—a group of warships under one command
hangar (HANG-ur)—a structure used to store planes
hull (HUHL)—the body of a ship
knot (NOT)—a measurement of speed for ships and boats; 1.15 miles per hour
missile (MISS-uhl)—an explosive that can fly

long distances

nuclear power (NOO-klee-ur POU-ur)—a powerful kind of energy that lasts longer than other kinds of energy

radar (RAY-dar)—machinery that uses radio waves to locate and guide things

runway (RUHN-way)—a road-like surface that planes use for taking off and landing

submarine (SUHB-muh-reen)—a ship that can travel both on top of water and underwater

torpedo (tor-PEE-doh)—an explosive that travels underwater

turbine (TUR-bine)—an engine powered by steam, water, or gas

warship (WOR-ship)—a ship with guns or other weapons that navies use for war

To Learn More

Asimov, Isaac and Elizabeth Kaplan. *How Do Big Ships Float?* Milwaukee: Gareth Stevens, 1993.

Garrison, Peter. *Carrier Aviation*. San Rafael, Calif.: Presidio Press, 1980.

Jordan, John. *Modern U.S. Navy*. New York: Salamander Books, 1986.

Preston, Antony. *Aircraft Carriers*. Minneapolis: Lerner, 1985.

Useful Addresses

Naval Historical Center
Washington Navy Yard
901 M Street SE
Washington, DC 20374-5060

USS *Lexington* Museum
2914 North Shoreline Boulevard
Corpus Christi, TX 78403-3076

USS *Yorktown*
Patriots Point Museum
40 Patriots Point Road
Mount Pleasant, SC 29464

Internet Sites

Navy Aircraft Carriers
http://www.nasni.navy.mil/carriers.html

Navy Fact File: Aircraft Carrier
http://www.navy.mil/navpalib/factfile/ships/ship
    cv.html

Navy: Welcome Aboard
http://www.navy.mil/

USS *Lexington* Museum
http://www.usslexington.com:80/vrmlpage.htm

Pilots make up part of an aircraft carrier's crew.

Index